JAMES *Polk*

JAMES *Polk*

OUR ELEVENTH PRESIDENT

By Ann Graham Gaines

SPIRIT
of America™

The Child's World®, Inc.
Chanhassen, Minnesota

9

JAMES *Polk*

Published in the United States of America by The Child's World®, Inc.
PO Box 326 • Chanhassen, MN 55317-0326 • 800-599-READ • www.childsworld.com

Acknowledgments

The Creative Spark: Mary Francis-DeMarois, Project Director; Elizabeth Sirimarco Budd, Series Editor; Robert Court, Design and Art Direction; Janine Graham, Page Layout; Jennifer Moyers, Production

The Child's World®, Inc.: Mary Berendes, Publishing Director; Red Line Editorial, Fact Research; Cindy Klingel, Curriculum Advisor; Robert Noyed, Historical Advisor

Photos

Cover: White House Collection, courtesy White House Historical Association; Courtesy Adams National Historical Park, Quincy, Massachusetts: 7; Amon Carter Museum, Fort Worth, Texas: 22 (Gift of Mrs. Anne Burnett Tandy in memory of her father, Thomas Loyd Burnett, 1870-1938), 27; Corbis: 9; Kevin Davidson: 25, 31; Denver Public Library Western History Department: 34; Courtesy George Eastman House: 32; Courtesy of The Hermitage, Nashville, Tennessee: 6, 12, 13, 14, 29, 30; James K. Polk Memorial State Historic Site: 8; Collections of the Library of Congress: 18, 21, 23, 24, 28, 35, 36, 37; Courtesy of the North Carolina Collections, University of North Carolina Library at Chapel Hill, 10, 15; Stock Montage: 33; Tennessee State Museum, Tennessee Historical Society Collection. Photography by June Dorman: 20; Tennessee State Museum Collection. Photography by June Dorman: 26

Registration

The Child's World®, Inc., Spirit of America™, and their associated logos are the sole property and registered trademarks of The Child's World®, Inc.

Library of Congress Cataloging-in-Publication Data

Gaines, Ann.
   James Polk : our eleventh president / by Ann Graham Gaines.
     p. cm.
   Includes bibliographical references and index.
    ISBN 1-56766-850-X (alk. paper)
   1. Polk, James K. (James Knox), 1795-1849—Juvenile literature. 2. Presidents—United States—
Biography—Juvenile literature. [1. Polk, James K. (James Knox), 1795–1849. 2. Presidents.] I. Title.
   E417 .G22 2001
   973.6'1'092—dc21

15   24   37

Contents

Chapter ONE

A Serious Boy

James Knox Polk was the nation's 11th president. He was a firm believer in "manifest destiny," the idea that the United States should expand all the way across the continent.

JAMES POLK, THE 11TH PRESIDENT OF THE United States, was a hard worker who almost always achieved what he set out to do. He was also a man with big ideas. He accomplished a great deal while he was president. His drive and determination came from his family.

James Polk was born on November 2, 1795, in Mecklenburg County, North Carolina. He was the first child born to Samuel and Jane Polk. The Polks owned a small farm. Samuel Polk spent his days working in the fields, growing and harvesting crops. Jane Polk took care of their home. Without modern machines to help, a home-maker's work was more difficult in those days. Mrs. Polk did laundry by hand and cooked meals over a fire.

Samuel Polk's parents lived nearby on another farm. The two families spent a great deal of time together and helped each other in any way they could. Jane and her mother-in-law canned fruits and vegetables together. Canning was a way of saving food harvested from the farm so that it could be eaten in the cold winter months. Samuel and his father, Ezekiel, helped each other harvest crops and build new barns.

The nation was still very young when James Polk was born. George Washington (above) was president, and the United States had declared its independence from Great Britain less than 20 years before.

James's mother went to church near their home every Sunday. James would grow up to share her belief in a stern God, who set strict rules for his people and punished sin. Yet James Polk never belonged to a church.

Historians know little about James Polk's childhood. He was often ill, which meant he could not attend school. His parents taught him reading, writing, and math to prepare him for when he was well enough to attend classes. James rarely played outside. Instead, he stayed in the family's cabin with his mother.

Polk lived in North Carolina for the first 10 years of his life. Today tourists can visit the site. The cabin where he lived was torn down long ago, but this one closely resembles it.

Interesting Facts

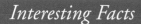

▶ When James Polk was a baby, his parents took him to church for baptism, a ceremony welcoming him into the church. When they arrived, the minister scolded James's father because he did not attend church services each Sunday. Samuel Polk said he did not have to go to church to have faith. They argued loudly until Samuel picked up James and stormed out of the church. The ceremony never took place.

When he felt well enough, he helped do chores and took care of his younger brothers and sisters.

In 1805, the Polk family moved to Tennessee. At the time, Tennessee was the frontier, land that only recently had been settled by Americans. James was almost 10 years old. His grandfather accompanied them on their trip. James's grandmother had died, so Ezekiel now lived with James's family. The move west was very exciting for the Polk children. Horses pulled the covered wagons that carried all their belongings. The trip took a long time because they traveled slowly. Often, they got out of the wagons and walked

8

alongside them. They crossed wide rivers and climbed through mountain passes. As they journeyed west, the roads became little more than dusty trails. Towns became smaller and were located farther apart. After 500 miles, the family finally reached their new home.

In Tennessee, Samuel and Ezekiel bought land near Nashville to start a farm. They built a new cabin and barn. They had to chop down trees to clear fields and put up fences. In the years that followed, Samuel Polk bought more and more land. Their small farm grew into a large **plantation.** He bought slaves to work in his fields.

Interesting Facts

▶ During James Polk's childhood, many people started to move west. For years, the Appalachian Mountains, which run south from Pennsylvania into northern Georgia, had marked the western edge of American settlement. They were too difficult to cross for most people. Then pioneers like Daniel Boone found mountain passes. Native Americans had used these narrow openings between the peaks for centuries. These paths made travel across the Appalachians much easier.

Life on the American frontier was difficult. Everyone in the family had to work together. Although James was often sick, he helped with the farm chores whenever he was able.

9

James Polk could not help with the farm work because he remained sick. He was not strong enough to work with a saw or a shovel. He also could not take part in the adventures that other frontier children enjoyed. He could not ramble through the woods or swim in cool rivers. Instead, he spent many days in bed. He was very serious, much like his parents and grandparents. Because there was no school near their home, Samuel and Jane educated all of their children, not just James. They gave them books to read and math problems to solve, and they also taught them **values.** The Polks wanted their children to work hard and lead a simple life. They also trained their family to stand up for their beliefs.

In 1812, when he was 17, James had surgery. In those days, some illnesses had different names. Historians are not completely sure what James had, but they know he had a terrible pain in his stomach. The operation made James well. After he recovered, he was able to go to school for the first time. He enrolled at a small school started by a local minister. Once James had learned everything he could from the minister, he went away to

10

live and study at a school in Murfreesboro, Tennessee. The classes he took there were more difficult. He studied Latin, literature, math, and science.

In 1816, when James Polk was 20, he enrolled at the University of North Carolina. He rode a horse hundreds of miles from his home in Tennessee to North Carolina. There he discovered that he already knew more than many of the other students. His professors decided he could start with second-year classes. His college studies and his membership in a **debating** club encouraged James's growing interest in law and government.

Polk had attended school for only three years before he enrolled at the University of North Carolina, shown below. He graduated with top honors and then returned to Tennessee with plans to become a lawyer.

Chapter TWO

A Political Career

James Polk graduated from college in 1818. He had been the best student in his class.

AFTER JAMES POLK GRADUATED FROM COLLEGE, he decided to become a lawyer. In those days, one did not go to law school to study law but went to work in a lawyer's office. Polk did so well at college that he could have gone to work for a lawyer in a large, busy, northern town, such as New York or Boston. But he missed his family, so he returned to Tennessee. He moved to the town of Columbia, where his parents had built a beautiful home. He went to work in nearby Nashville in the office of a well-known attorney. Nashville is the state capital of Tennessee. Polk met many state lawmakers there. He soon became interested in **politics.** In 1819, he became the clerk in the state senate. In this position, he acted as a secretary, keeping the senate records.

In 1820, Polk passed his law exams and opened his own office in Columbia. He quickly became busy and successful. At the same time, he led an active social life. In 1821, he met a young woman named Sarah Childress. Her father was a wealthy planter and an important man in Tennessee. Sarah was a lively, intelligent woman who had a fine education. The two young people began seeing a great deal of each other.

Polk continued to work as the state senate's clerk until 1822. He also developed his own political goals. Sarah Childress encouraged his growing interest in politics.

By 1816, the Polk family ran a very successful farm. Samuel Polk built this beautiful brick house in Columbia, Tennessee, while James was away at college. After he graduated, James returned to live there. He stayed with his family until he married in 1824.

13

Polk soon decided he wanted to run for elected office. By this time, he was a man of 27. He was serious, dedicated, and stood up for his beliefs.

In 1823, the people of Tennessee elected James Polk to their state **legislature.** He also continued to work as a lawyer. The following January, he married Sarah Childress. Sarah was pleased with his success, even though she understood he would have to spend a great deal of time working, both in his law office and in the legislature. Over the years, Sarah helped James in his career. She read newspapers and documents for him. She also wrote letters for him.

In 1824, Polk was elected to the House of Representatives, which is part of the U.S. Congress. He was a member of the Democratic Party, a powerful U.S. **political party**. He and Sarah moved to Washington, D.C., and Polk quickly became active in the House.

14

He liked to debate important issues of the day, issues that affected the entire country. He also introduced many **bills.**

Although his own career in Washington had barely begun, Polk soon became close friends with one of the nation's best known political leaders, Andrew Jackson. Jackson was then a U.S. senator. Like Polk, he was a Democrat, and he also came from Tennessee. In 1824, Jackson ran for president but lost. He won the next election, however, and the one after that as well. Jackson was president from 1829 to 1837. During this period, he and Polk formed a friendship that lasted for life. They were political **allies.** Polk helped Jackson in the House of Representatives. He urged other members to vote for laws the president wanted passed. Jackson helped Polk meet other important politicians.

Polk worked at the State Capitol of Tennessee for many years, first as a clerk for the senate and later as a lawmaker. In 1824, he entered national politics when he was elected to the House of Representatives.

The people of Tennessee reelected James Polk to the House of Representatives six times. He and Sarah enjoyed life in the busy

After Polk was elected to the U.S. House of Representatives, he met Andrew Jackson (above). The two men both came from Tennessee and shared many of the same beliefs. When Jackson became president in 1829, he and Polk helped each other achieve their goals.

Interesting Facts

▶ When Polk ran for governor of Tennessee, Mrs. Polk worked to get him elected. She mailed information to voters, arranged schedules, and wrote letters.

capital city. Over the years, he became a respected leader. He served on the Ways and Means committee. This committee decides how the government should spend its money.

In 1835, James Polk became the Speaker of the House. The Speaker takes charge of the activities in the House of Representatives. The other members elect the Speaker. This position gave Polk a great deal of power, but he felt frustrated. He had decided that he wanted to become president one day. Although congressmen regard the Speaker as a powerful man, most American citizens do not understand how important the position is. Polk knew the public needed to know him better before he could win a national election.

To accomplish this, Polk decided he would first try to achieve a lesser goal—to become a governor. In 1839, he left the House of Representatives. He and Sarah returned to Tennessee. There they lived on his family's plantation, which now belonged to him. Within months, Polk ran for governor of Tennessee and won.

This new office quickly won fame for Polk. In fact, he expected the Democratic Party to choose him as the **candidate** for vice president in the 1840 election. This did not happen. The Democratic Party had many difficulties at the time. Its leaders could not agree on who should run for president. The party finally **nominated** Martin Van Buren but chose no one for vice president. The nomination would not have helped Polk, for Van Buren lost the election.

Washington, D.C., was still a rural community when the Polks moved there. They enjoyed the social life in the city, as well as the success that James had in his career. Even so, he decided the best way to achieve his political goals was to run for governor in his home state.

18

JAMES POLK BEGAN SERVING IN THE U.S. CONGRESS IN 1825. AT THAT TIME, large numbers of American settlers began moving to Texas, which was then part of Mexico. The Mexican government granted an American named Moses Austin a large piece of land there in 1821. His son, Stephen, went to Texas to take possession of the land. Soon 5,000 Americans had come to live in the colony he established. Mexico allowed other Americans to establish colonies in Texas, too. By 1830, 25,000 Americans had moved there. These settlers quickly gained power in the local governments.

Throughout Polk's term in Congress, Texas made headlines in U.S. newspapers. At first, Americans read of the opportunities Texas offered. There were vast spreads of open land. People could build large farms for very little money. There were also rumors that silver might be found there. In 1835, the biggest news of all arrived. Texas was on the verge of war. The Mexican government decided it wanted more control over the American settlers who lived in Texas. A small group of Mexican soldiers went to Gonzales, Texas, a town settled by Americans. The soldiers demanded the Americans return a cannon the Mexican government had given them. A battle followed that marked the beginning of what would become a **revolution.** Perhaps the most famous battle of all took place at the Alamo, shown at left. About 3,000 Mexican soldiers attacked the Texans, who were using the former church as a fort. For 13 days, more than 180 Texan soldiers held off their attackers. But the Mexicans finally succeeded in taking over the Alamo and killing all the Texans. At least 1,000 Mexican soldiers died in the battle as well.

Chapter THREE

Texas and Oregon

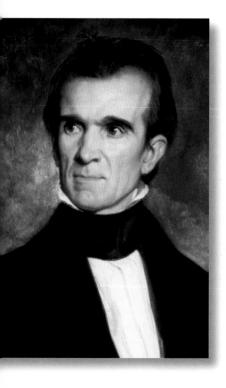

Polk hoped to run for vice president in the election of 1844, but Andrew Jackson suggested the Democrats select him as their presidential candidate instead.

POLK REMAINED GOVERNOR OF TENNESSEE until 1841. He ran for reelection that year but lost. He and Sarah went home to their plantation, although he did not devote much attention to running it. He wanted to run for governor again. The next election was held in 1843, but Polk lost that election as well.

A presidential election took place in 1844. Polk hoped once more to run as vice president, but events took an unexpected turn. The Democrats decided they did not want Martin Van Buren to run for president. This was mainly because he did not want Texas to become part of the United States. Texas was an independent **republic.** Until 1836, it had belonged to Mexico. Then the Texas Revolution broke out. Texans, including American settlers and Mexican citizens, fought for independence.

For a time, it seemed the small Texan army could not win. The army Mexico had sent to fight was larger and had better weapons. The Texans' cause seemed lost when they were defeated at the Battle of the Alamo on March 6, 1836. But General Sam Houston rallied his soldiers and defeated the Mexicans at the Battle of San Jacinto one month later. They captured Mexican General Antonio Lopez de Santa Anna, who had led the attack on the Alamo.

After the battle, the Mexican army gave up. Texas became its own country, an independent republic. Almost 10 years after the revolution had ended, most Texans wanted to join the United States. Many Southerners were also eager to see it join the **Union** because Texas allowed slavery. If Congress voted to admit Texas, it would mean that its members wanted slavery to remain legal in the United States.

Martin Van Buren, the nation's eighth president, was not reelected for a second term. But he hoped to try again in the election of 1844. The Democrats did not choose him as their candidate, but selected James Polk instead.

The Alamo was originally a mission, a church built by Christians in San Antonio, Texas. Texan soldiers fighting for independence captured San Antonio in December of 1835. The Alamo was no longer a church by that time. But it still had several buildings with thick, strong walls. The Texans decided to use it as a fort. In 1836, Mexican General Santa Anna led an army into San Antonio. They surrounded the Texan soldiers in the Alamo. After 13 days, the Mexicans stormed the walls, killing more than 180 Texans inside.

People still asked Andrew Jackson for his advice, although he no longer worked in politics. He suggested the Democrats ask James Polk to run for president. Polk had made it clear that he believed Texas should join the Union immediately. The party took Jackson's advice, and Polk agreed to seek the office.

During his presidential **campaign,** Polk talked about his hope to see the country expand. He thought new land would make the United States even stronger and more powerful. He was in favor of admitting not only Texas to the Union, but the Oregon **Territory** as well.

22

Today Oregon is a state located north of California on the Pacific Ocean. In James Polk's day, a much larger area was called Oregon. From east to west, it stretched from the Rocky Mountains to the Pacific. North and south, it lay between the 42nd **parallel** and just over the 54th parallel at 54 degrees, 40 minutes.

General Sam Houston (left) led the Texans in the Battle of San Jacinto. As they rushed into battle, they cried, "Remember the Alamo!" They defeated 1,200 Mexican soldiers and captured their general. Houston later became the president of the Republic of Texas.

A print made during Polk's campaign shows him (in the upper right corner) welcoming Texas into the Union. Sam Houston is at the head of the boat. Opponents of the movement to accept Texas into the Union are dragged through the water as Polk achieves his goal.

Degrees and minutes are measurements used to define distances. In other words, it stretched from California all the way to Alaska, which then belonged to Russia.

Spanish explorers had been the first Europeans to arrive in the Oregon Territory. It was wild, wooded, and beautiful, a land inhabited by many Native Americans. The Spanish had claimed the territory for their king in the 1700s. In 1792, Spain gave its claim to Great Britain.

Many animals lived in Oregon. For centuries, Native Americans had hunted otters and other creatures for food and fur. Later British and then American fur-trading

24

companies sent traders and trappers to the area. The animal skins they trapped could be sold for a great deal of money. The region was very valuable, and nobody was willing to give it up. In 1818, a **treaty** declared that the British and Americans would share the Oregon Territory.

For many years, the United States had asked Britain to turn over all of the territory south of the 49th parallel. Britain always refused, and Americans were growing angry.

The Oregon Territory stretched from the Rocky Mountains all the way to the Pacific Ocean. It lay between the 42nd parallel to the south and the 54th parallel to the north. For years, Britain refused to turn over to the United States the land between the 49th parallel and the Columbia River. Many Americans, including James Polk, said the nation should fight to take over all land below the Alaskan border, which lay at 54 degrees, 40 minutes. During Polk's campaign, a popular rallying cry was, "Fifty-four forty or fight!"

During his campaign, Polk said he wanted to see Britain give up its entire claim to Oregon, not just the region below the 49th parallel. One of his campaign slogans was "Fifty-four forty or fight." This meant he believed Americans should fight to win the entire territory between California and Alaska— everything below 54 degrees, 40 minutes.

Many Americans agreed with Polk's **expansionist** views. They, too, wanted to see the nation grow larger. It was a difficult election, but Polk defeated his opponent. He was on his way to the White House.

Polk, shown here speaking to the people of Tennessee, made expansion into the western parts of the continent the main issue of his campaign.

PRESIDENT POLK WAS DETERMINED THAT THE UNITED STATES MUST TAKE CONTROL of California. He wanted this region because it held untold riches that would greatly benefit the nation.

In the 16th century, Spanish explorers became the first Europeans to see this beautiful region. They had claimed the land for their king. In 1769, Spain began to send missionaries and soldiers to build churches and forts there. They wrote letters describing the wonderful climate and how many fruits and vegetables could be grown.

Soon Great Britain, Russia, and the United States all wanted to possess California. This was not only because it could be settled and farmed, but also because there were many animals that could be trapped for fur. Captains of ships that ventured to California reported that there were many safe ports along the coast as well. In James Polk's day, the United States wanted to start trading with Asian countries such as China and Japan. Polk and other politicians realized that this would be much easier if the United States owned territory on the Pacific Ocean.

Chapter FOUR

President Polk

Polk was 49 years old when he became president. He was the youngest president up to that time.

JAMES POLK'S **INAUGURATION** TOOK PLACE ON March 4, 1845. He was a strong leader. From the beginning, he worked with Congress to achieve the Democratic Party's goals. They wanted to establish a treasury, a national department that would handle the nation's money matters. They hoped to cut back on the amount of money the government spent on roads, bridges, and canals. Finally, they wanted to lower tariffs, which are taxes placed on goods from other countries. Lowering tariffs would make it cheaper for Americans to buy these goods.

Polk's major goal was to see the United States grow in size. Three days before he entered office, President John Tyler had signed an act that made Texas part of the United States.

This meant Polk could devote his attention to other parts of the continent. Americans began to talk about "manifest destiny," the nation's right to spread across the entire continent. Polk's two biggest goals were to take control of Oregon and California. He felt these two western territories would bring valuable new resources to the Union. Resources are valuable things in nature, such as water or minerals.

One of the first tasks a new president faces is the selection of a cabinet. A cabinet is the group of people who help a president make important decisions. Polk (seated second from right) and his cabinet posed for this photograph in 1845. It was the first photograph ever taken inside the White House.

Sarah Polk acted as her husband's personal secretary when he was president. She also wrote his letters. Neither of the Polks ever took a day of vacation while he was in office.

First, Polk sent a message to Great Britain, offering to split the Oregon Territory in two. Britain would take one part of it, and the United States would take the other. The British refused his offer, so the U.S. government declared it would no longer honor their agreement to share the region.

British leaders feared the United States would go to war to take over the territory. That would have cost too much money and too many lives. They finally agreed to make the 49th parallel the border between U.S. and British lands. This gave the United States the region that is now the states of Oregon and Washington. Canada, which was then a British colony, would keep the land south of Alaska. That region is now the province of British Columbia. A province is a main division within Canada, much like a state in the United States.

The United States grew much bigger during Polk's time in office. The yellow and green areas in the map below show land obtained during his presidency, as well as Texas, which was obtained just before he entered office.

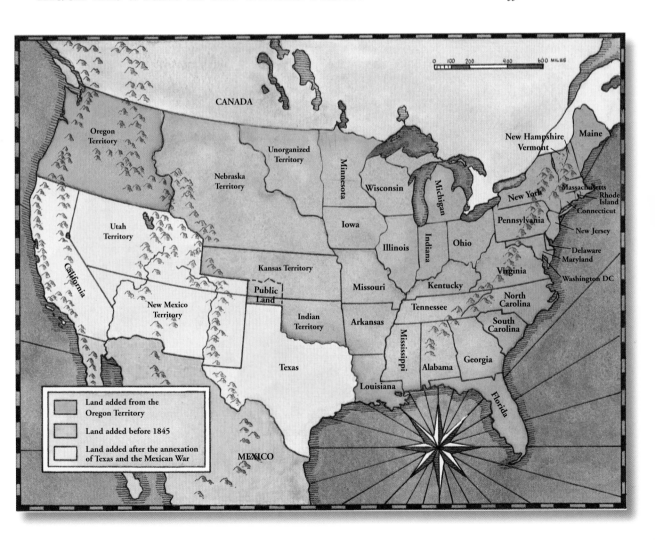

CANADA

Oregon Territory

Unorganized Territory

New Hampshire
Vermont

Maine

Nebraska Territory

Minnesota

Wisconsin

Michigan

New York

Massachusetts

Rhode Island

Utah Territory

Iowa

Connecticut

Pennsylvania

New Jersey

California

Illinois

Indiana

Ohio

Delaware
Maryland

Kansas Territory

Missouri

Kentucky

Virginia

Washington DC

Public Land

New Mexico Territory

Indian Territory

Arkansas

Tennessee

North Carolina

South Carolina

Texas

Mississippi

Alabama

Georgia

Louisiana

Florida

Land added from the Oregon Territory

Land added before 1845

Land added after the annexation of Texas and the Mexican War

MEXICO

0 100 200 400 600 MILES

The Polks posed for this photograph outside the White House with friends and other politicians. Barely visible at far left is another future president, James Buchanan. To Polk's right is Dolley Madison, the wife of the nation's fourth president, James Madison.

Polk wanted the United States to grow even more. He wanted it to control California, which belonged to Mexico. He knew it was a rich land, well suited for settlement and farming. The Mexican government had been very angry when Texas joined the United States. Polk realized that Mexico would not peacefully agree to hand over California. He decided it was worth fighting for. He sent thousands of American soldiers to Texas, and they prepared to invade Mexico.

The U.S. soldiers camped along the Rio Grande River, the boundary between the United States and Mexico. President Polk wanted a war to break out, but he hoped the United States would not have to start it. He wanted Mexico to be so angry at the presence of an American army on its border that it would fight to drive it away.

For a long time, Mexico failed to attack. Polk thought the United States might have to

Interesting Facts

▸ Abraham Lincoln, then a young politician, opposed the Mexican War. He thought Polk and his supporters were fighting to bring more slave states into the Union.

During the Mexican War, American soldiers were often outnumbered. The Mexican forces were strong. But against all odds, Americans forged ahead, determined to win the war.

start the war. At the last moment, he received a message. Mexican troops had fired on American soldiers. Congress declared war on Mexico in May of 1846, just as the president had wanted.

Not all Americans supported the war. Many people in the North did not want their country to fight Mexico. They did not want the United States to add more land until Congress decided whether slavery would be legal in new states. People also complained because the war would cost money, and too many soldiers would lose their lives.

Toward the end of Polk's presidency, people began journeying to one of the nation's newest territories, California. They hoped to strike it rich, for gold had just been discovered there. The Gold Rush would continue for many years, as people traveled to California dreaming of a new life.

The Mexican War continued for a year and a half. The American army invaded Mexico and won many victories. Finally, it **occupied** the capital, Mexico City. In 1848, Mexico agreed to the Treaty of Guadalupe Hidalgo, which gave the United States land that would become the states of Arizona, Nevada, California, Utah, and parts of New Mexico, Colorado, and Wyoming.

The treaty added nearly 1.2 million square miles to the Union. Polk regarded this as his greatest achievement. Americans also praised him at the war's end.

The very year California became part of the United States, gold was discovered there. The news traveled by ship to the eastern United States. One of the first shipments of gold nuggets was sent to President Polk. In the years that followed, Americans, as well as people from many other countries, flocked to California. They hoped to strike it rich.

When he ran for president in 1844, Polk had promised he would serve only one term as president. He kept this promise. He was very popular at the end of the war, but he did not run for reelection in 1848. Tired and ill, Polk was ready to leave the task of running the nation to someone else. Just before he left office, Polk wrote about his time as president: "They have been four years of … labor and anxiety. I am heartily rejoiced that my

As he had promised, Polk did not run for reelection in 1848. He was tired and ready to give up the great responsibilities of the presidency.

General Zachary Taylor had become a hero in the Mexican War. Americans credited him with the victory over Mexico, and he easily won the presidential election of 1848. He had a short presidency, however. He died in office after just 16 months.

term is so near its close." A hero named Zachary Taylor had gained fame as a general during the Mexican War. He was elected president and took office in 1849.

After Taylor's inauguration, the Polks returned to Tennessee. James Polk was tired. He had been working too hard for a long time. He had never taken a single day of vacation. A lack of rest had left him weak. Just three months after his return home, he became sick. His exhausted body could not fight off his illness. He died just three months after returning to Tennessee, at the age of 53.

James Polk had been a hardworking and determined man. As president, he had fulfilled his great goal, helping the country grow much larger in size. His vision and strength allowed the United States to stretch across the continent.

ABOUT 100,000 AMERICAN SOLDIERS FOUGHT IN THE MEXICAN WAR. ALTHOUGH fewer than 2,000 of them died in battle, the war was terrible for all. It began on the Rio Grande, the river on the border between Texas and Mexico. In battle after battle, the American troops were outnumbered. Most of these battles took place on Mexican soil, which gave the enemy an advantage. The U.S. Navy carried some soldiers to Mexico on boats. But most marched hundreds of miles across hot, dry deserts.

In those days, soldiers still fought with swords as well as guns. Battles could be very bloody. American soldiers also suffered from serious diseases. More than 11,000 men died from disease, and many more than died in battle. Soldiers' families knew the real cost of the war. Even so, most Americans rejoiced over the victory. The United States gained 1.2 million square miles of land at the war's end.

37

1795 James Polk is born on November 2 in North Carolina.

1805 The Polk family moves to Tennessee.

1812 Polk undergoes a dangerous operation. After he recovers, he is healthy enough to go to school for the first time.

1816 Polk enrolls at the University of North Carolina.

1818 Polk graduates from college after just two years of study. He returns home to Tennessee where he studies law with a well-known lawyer.

1819 Polk takes a job as clerk to the Tennessee State Senate.

1821 Polk finishes his law studies. He becomes a lawyer and opens his own law office in Columbia, Tennessee. He begins to court Sarah Childress.

1822 Polk resigns his position as clerk for the state senate.

1823 Polk is elected to the Tennessee state legislature.

1824 Polk marries Sarah Childress. Polk is elected to the U.S. House of Representatives. He and Sarah Polk move to Washington, D.C.

1826 Polk is reelected to the House. He goes on to be reelected five more times.

1828 Andrew Jackson is elected president. Polk and Jackson become political allies. Over the years, Jackson helps Polk meet important politicians. Polk helps Jackson pass bills in the House.

1835 Members of Congress elect Polk to the important position of Speaker of the House.

1836 After the Texans win their independence from Mexico, they establish the Republic of Texas, an independent nation.

1837 Martin Van Buren is inaugurated president on March 4.

1839 Polk leaves the House of Representatives. He and Sarah return to Tennessee, where he is elected governor.

1840 The Democrats lose the presidential election to Whig candidate William Henry Harrison.

1841 Polk runs for reelection as governor of Tennessee, but loses. President Harrison dies after only one month in office. His vice president, John Tyler, becomes president.

1843 Polk runs for election as governor of Tennessee, but loses once again.

1844 The Democratic Party, in a surprise move, nominates Polk as its presidential candidate. During the campaign, he supports the expansion of the United States into the West. He promises to support the annexation of Texas. He wins the election.

1845 Texas gives up its status as an independent nation and joins the United States just a few days before Polk becomes president. Polk is inaugurated on March 4. He immediately begins to negotiate with Great Britain for the Oregon Territory. The United States fights with Mexico over the southern border of Texas.

1846 Great Britain agrees to turn over to the United States all land south of the 49th parallel in the Oregon Territory. In May, the Mexican War begins. Earlier Polk sent U.S. soldiers to Texas, hoping for war to break out. He hopes to win Mexico's rich land in California.

1847 Americans capture Mexico City, which will end the Mexican War.

1848 In February, the Treaty of Guadalupe Hidalgo with Mexico gives the United States nearly 1.2 million square miles of western land and firmly establishes the border between Mexico and Texas. Gold is discovered in California in March. By August, news of the discovery has reached the eastern United States. Polk decides not to run for a second term as president. War hero Zachary Taylor is elected president in the November election.

1849 In January, Polk receives a package containing gold nuggets from California. When the news spreads, the Gold Rush begins. Zachary Taylor is inaugurated president in March. James and Sarah Polk return home to Tennessee. James Polk dies there on June 15, at the age of 53.

allies (AL-lize)
Allies are people or groups of people who help each other by working toward a common goal. Jackson and Polk were political allies.

bills (BILZ)
Bills are ideas for new laws that are presented to a group of lawmakers. Polk introduced many bills to the House of Representatives.

campaign (kam-PAYN)
A campaign is the process of running for an election, including activities such as giving speeches or attending rallies. Polk focused on expansionism during his campaign.

candidate (KAN-dih-det)
A candidate is a person running in an election. Polk hoped the Democratic Party would choose him as its candidate for vice president in 1840.

debating (dih-BAY-ting)
Debating is the discussion of a question or topic, considering reasons for and against it. Polk joined a debating club in college.

expansionist (ek-SPAN-shun-ist)
An expansionist is a person who wants to increase the size of something.

Polk was an expansionist because he wanted the United States to grow.

historians (hih-STOR-ee-unz)
Historians are people who are experts in history. Historians do not know very much about Polk's childhood.

inauguration (ih-nawg-yuh-RAY-shun)
An inauguration is the ceremony that takes place when a new president begins a term. Polk's inauguration took place on March 4, 1845.

legislature (LEJ-uh-slay-chur)
A legislature is the part of a government that makes laws. Polk was elected to the Tennessee state legislature in 1823.

nominate (NOM-ih-nayt)
If a political party nominates someone, it chooses him or her to run for a political office. The Democrats nominated Martin Van Buren as their presidential candidate in 1840.

occupied (AHK-yeh-pyd)
If a place has been occupied, it has been taken over by force. American soldiers occupied Mexico City during the Mexican War.

40

parallel (PAIR-eh-lel)
A parallel is an imaginary line that circles the Earth and is used on maps and globes for measurement. The parallels are equal spaces apart from each other and measure distance from the equator.

plantation (plan-TAY-shun)
A plantation is a large farm or group of farms that grows crops such as tobacco, sugarcane, or cotton. The Polk's small farm grew into a large plantation.

**political party
(puh-LIT-uh-kul PAR-tee)**
A political party is a group of people who share similar ideas about how to run a government. Polk was a member of the Democratic political party.

politics (PAWL-uh-tiks)
Politics refers to the actions and practices of the government. Polk became interested in politics while he was studying to become a lawyer.

republic (ree-PUB-lik)
A republic is a nation with a government elected by its citizens. Texas was an independent republic after the Texas Revolution.

revolution (rev-uh-LOO-shun)
A revolution is something that causes a complete change in government. Texas fought a revolution to win its independence from Mexico in 1836.

territory (TAIR-uh-tor-ee)
A territory is a land or region, especially land that belongs to a government. Polk wanted the Oregon Territory to become part of the United States.

treaty (TREE-tee)
A treaty is a formal agreement between nations. In 1818, a treaty declared that the British and Americans would share the Oregon Territory.

union (YOON-yen)
A union is the joining together of two people or groups of people, such as states. The Union is another name for the United States.

values (VAL-yooz)
Values are the beliefs by which a person lives. Polk's values included hard work and speaking up for what he believed.

Our PRESIDENTS

President	Birthplace	Life Span	Presidency	Political Party	First Lady
George Washington	Virginia	1732–1799	1789–1797	None	Martha Dandridge Custis Washington
John Adams	Massachusetts	1735–1826	1797–1801	Federalist	Abigail Smith Adams
Thomas Jefferson	Virginia	1743–1826	1801–1809	Democratic-Republican	widower
James Madison	Virginia	1751–1836	1809–1817	Democratic Republican	Dolley Payne Todd Madison
James Monroe	Virginia	1758–1831	1817–1825	Democratic Republican	Elizabeth Kortright Monroe
John Quincy Adams	Massachusetts	1767–1848	1825–1829	Democratic-Republican	Louisa Johnson Adams
Andrew Jackson	South Carolina	1767–1845	1829–1837	Democrat	widower
Martin Van Buren	New York	1782–1862	1837–1841	Democrat	widower
William H. Harrison	Virginia	1773–1841	1841	Whig	Anna Symmes Harrison
John Tyler	Virginia	1790–1862	1841–1845	Whig	Letitia Christian Tyler / Julia Gardiner Tyler
James K. Polk	North Carolina	1795–1849	1845–1849	Democrat	Sarah Childress Polk

Our PRESIDENTS

President	Birthplace	Life Span	Presidency	Political Party	First Lady
Zachary Taylor	Virginia	1784–1850	1849–1850	Whig	Margaret Mackall Smith Taylor
Millard Fillmore	New York	1800–1874	1850–1853	Whig	Abigail Powers Fillmore
Franklin Pierce	New Hampshire	1804–1869	1853–1857	Democrat	Jane Means Appleton Pierce
James Buchanan	Pennsylvania	1791–1868	1857–1861	Democrat	never married
Abraham Lincoln	Kentucky	1809–1865	1861–1865	Republican	Mary Todd Lincoln
Andrew Johnson	North Carolina	1808–1875	1865–1869	Democrat	Eliza McCardle Johnson
Ulysses S. Grant	Ohio	1822–1885	1869–1877	Republican	Julia Dent Grant
Rutherford B. Hayes	Ohio	1822–1893	1877–1881	Republican	Lucy Webb Hayes
James A. Garfield	Ohio	1831–1881	1881	Republican	Lucretia Rudolph Garfield
Chester A. Arthur	Vermont	1829–1886	1881–1885	Republican	widower
Grover Cleveland	New Jersey	1837–1908	1885–1889	Democrat	Frances Folsom Cleveland

Our PRESIDENTS

President	Birthplace	Life Span	Presidency	Political Party	First Lady
Benjamin Harrison	Ohio	1833–1901	1889–1893	Republican	Caroline Scott Harrison
Grover Cleveland	New Jersey	1837–1908	1893–1897	Democrat	Frances Folsom Cleveland
William McKinley	Ohio	1843–1901	1897–1901	Republican	Ida Saxton McKinley
Theodore Roosevelt	New York	1858–1919	1901–1909	Republican	Edith Kermit Carow Roosevelt
William H. Taft	Ohio	1857–1930	1909–1913	Republican	Helen Herron Taft
Woodrow Wilson	Virginia	1856–1924	1913–1921	Democrat	Ellen L. Axson Wilson Edith Bolling Galt Wilson
Warren G. Harding	Ohio	1865–1923	1921–1923	Republican	Florence Kling De Wolfe Harding
Calvin Coolidge	Vermont	1872–1933	1923–1929	Republican	Grace Goodhue Coolidge
Herbert C. Hoover	Iowa	1874–1964	1929–1933	Republican	Lou Henry Hoover
Franklin D. Roosevelt	New York	1882–1945	1933–1945	Democrat	Anna Eleanor Roosevelt Roosevelt
Harry S. Truman	Missouri	1884–1972	1945–1953	Democrat	Elizabeth Wallace Truman

Our PRESIDENTS

President	Birthplace	Life Span	Presidency	Political Party	First Lady
Dwight D. Eisenhower	Texas	1890–1969	1953–1961	Republican	Mary "Mamie" Doud Eisenhower
John F. Kennedy	Massachusetts	1917–1963	1961–1963	Democrat	Jacqueline Bouvier Kennedy
Lyndon B. Johnson	Texas	1908–1973	1963–1969	Democrat	Claudia Alta Taylor Johnson
Richard M. Nixon	California	1913–1994	1969–1974	Republican	Thelma Catherine Ryan Nixon
Gerald Ford	Nebraska	1913–	1974–1977	Republican	Elizabeth "Betty" Bloomer Warren Ford
James Carter	Georgia	1924–	1977–1981	Democrat	Rosalynn Smith Carter
Ronald Reagan	Illinois	1911–	1981–1989	Republican	Nancy Davis Reagan
George Bush	Massachusetts	1924–	1989–1993	Republican	Barbara Pierce Bush
William Clinton	Arkansas	1946–	1993–2001	Democrat	Hillary Rodham Clinton
George W. Bush	Connecticut	1946–	2001–	Republican	Laura Welch Bush

Presidential FACTS

Qualifications
To run for president, a candidate must
- be at least 35 years old
- be a citizen who was born in the United States
- have lived in the United States for 14 years

Term of Office
A president's term of office is four years. No president can stay in office for more than two terms.

Election Date
The presidential election takes place every four years on the first Tuesday of November.

Inauguration Date
Presidents are inaugurated on January 20.

Oath of Office
I do solemnly swear I will faithfully execute the office of the President of the United States and will to the best of my ability preserve, protect, and defend the Constitution of the United States.

Write a Letter to the President
One of the best things about being a U.S. citizen is that Americans get to participate in their government. They can speak out if they feel government leaders aren't doing their jobs. They can also praise leaders who are going the extra mile. Do you have something you'd like the president to do? Should the president worry more about the environment and encourage people to recycle? Should the government spend more money on our schools? You can write a letter to the president to say how you feel!

1600 Pennsylvania Avenue
Washington, D.C. 20500

You can even send an e-mail to: president@whitehouse.gov

For Further INFORMATION

Internet Sites

See James K. Polk's boyhood home in Tennessee and read more about his family at the James K. Polk Memorial Association's Web site:
http://www.jameskpolk.com

Read a discussion of Polk's achievements:
http://www.users.nac.net/tderosa/polk.html

Find more information on Sarah Childress Polk at the White House's first ladies site:
http://www.whitehouse.gov/WH/glimpse/firstladies/html/sp11.html

Learn more about Polk's role in Texas history:
http://www.lsjunction.com/people/polk.html

Learn more about all the presidents and visit the White House:
http://www.whitehouse.gov/WH/glimpse/presidents/html/presidents.html
http://www.thepresidency.org/presinfo.htm
http://www.americanpresidents.org/

Books

Collier, Christopher. *Hispanic America, Texas, and the Mexican War, 1835–1850.* New York: Benchmark, 1998.

Jacobs, William Jay. *War with Mexico* (Spotlight on American History). Brookfield, CT: Millbrook Press, 1993.

Lindop, Edmund. *James K. Polk, Abraham Lincoln, and Theodore Roosevelt.* New York: Twenty-First Century Books, 1995.

Tibbitts, Alison. *James K. Polk.* Springfield, NJ: Enslow, 1999.

Van Leeuwen, Jean. *Bound for Oregon.* New York: Dial, 1994.

Index